STEP RIGHT UP

How Doc and Jim Key
Taught the World About Kindness

by Donna Janell Bowman • illustrated by Daniel Minter

Lee & Low Books Inc. • New York

Acknowledgments

This book would not exist without the years-long support of many champions. For their research assistance and resources, many thanks go to the staffs of the Tennessee State Library and Archives, the Shelbyville Public Library, and the Round Rock Public Library. Many thanks to my agent, Erin Murphy, for believing in me and this project; my editors, Samantha Wolf and Louise May, for their expert guidance in shaping Doc and Jim's story; Daniel Minter, for bringing Doc and Jim to life with such exquisite art; Lee & Low Books, for its support of diversity in children's literature; and the village of friends, coaches, and colleagues who raised me through the process of this book. Special winks and nods to my most steadfast and encouraging critiquers: Carmen Oliver, Don Tate, Bethany Hegedus, Shana Burg, Samantha Clark, Cynthia Levinson, Shelley Ann Jackson, Amy Farrier, Marsha Riti, Chris Barton, and Cynthia Leitich Smith. Especial gratitude and love to my husband, Chris, and to my sons, Justin and Ethan, who supported me and sustained me in countless ways. This book would not be possible without them. —D.J.B.

Special thanks to Susan Gordon, archivist at the Tennessee State Library and Archives; Carolyn Merino Mullin, founder and executive director, Museum of Animals; and Edith Campbell, assistant librarian, Indiana State University, for reviewing this story and for their valuable input.

Photograph of William "Doc" Key on the first page of the Afterword from *The Story of Beautiful Jim Key: The Most Wonderful Horse in All the World* by Albert R. Rogers, 1901 (public domain material). All other photographs in the Afterword courtesy of the Tennessee State Library and Archives, Nashville, Tennessee.

Book design by David and Susan Neuhaus/NeuStudio • Book production by The Kids at Our House
The text is set in Berling • The illustrations are rendered as linoleum block prints painted with acrylic
Manufactured in China by Jade Productions, July 2016
Printed on paper from responsible sources
First Edition   10 9 8 7 6 5 4 3 2 1
Library of Congress Cataloging-in-Publication Data
Names: Bowman, Donna Janell, author. | Minter, Daniel, illustrator.
Title: Step right up : how Doc and Jim Key taught the world about kindness / by Donna Janell Bowman ; illustrated by Daniel Minter.
Description: First edition. | New York, NY : Lee & Low Books Inc., [2016] | Summary: "A picture book biography of Dr. William Key, a former slave and self-trained veterinarian who taught his horse, Jim, to read and write and who together with Jim became one of the most famous traveling performance acts around the turn of the twentieth century. Includes afterword and author's sources"— Provided by publisher.
Identifiers: LCCN 2015030604 | ISBN 9781620141489 (hardcover : alk. paper)
Subjects: LCSH: Key, Bill, 1833-1909—Juvenile literature. | Beautiful Jim Key (Horse)—Juvenile literature. | Humane education—United States—History—Juvenile literature. | Horses—Training—United States—History—Juvenile literature. | Horse trainers—United States—Biography—Juvenile literature. | Human-animal communication—United States—Juvenile literature. | Human-animal relationships—United States—Juvenile literature.
Classification: LCC HV4712 .B723 2016 | DDC 179/.3—dc23
LC record available at http://lccn.loc.gov/2015030604

To my mother, who shared her love of horses with me —*D.J.B.*

To Kristie Rosende, the greatest art teacher ever! —*D.M.*

Spring 1889 stretched a blanket of wildflowers over Shelbyville, Tennessee, but William "Doc" Key barely noticed. He paced and fidgeted like an expectant father. He had been on hand for plenty of births before, but this one was special. Visions of a future champion racehorse darted through his mind as he comforted his mare Lauretta. Finally a dark, wet colt lay shivering at her side.

Doc knelt to welcome the little fellow, but something was terribly wrong. "He's the most spindly, shank-legged animal I ever did see," he said.

Most folks would have given up on the colt right then. But Doc had a kind streak that ran clear through his heart and all the way back to his childhood.

William Key was born into slavery in 1833. As a child in Shelbyville, he was full of questions about the world.

In some parts of the United States, educating an enslaved person was a crime. Even where it was not forbidden, many owners did not want their enslaved people to be educated. But John and Martha Key, William's masters, like several others in Shelbyville, thought differently. So the Keys allowed William to join their sons for lessons.

Learning gave William a sense of freedom.

From the time William was about six years old, it was clear he had a special way with animals. No matter how wild or rascally the animals, William befriended them and tamed them. He especially loved horses.

A few years later, William's masters started sending him across Bedford County to work with other farmers' ornery animals. During these travels, William saw how some animals were neglected, beaten, and worked to death. He was gentle and patient with them instead. He thought nothing was worse than being hurtful.

William learned all he could about caring for the injuries and illnesses of
animals and people. He paid special attention when his mother taught him
how to distill roots and herbs into homemade remedies. As William worked
at different farms and businesses, his doctoring skills developed, and his
reputation grew across Tennessee. By the time he was a young man, William
was so good at treating injuries and ailments that everyone started calling
him Doc Key, or just Doc.

In 1865 the Civil War ended, and Doc built a new life as a free man. He married and bought his first patch of land in Shelbyville. It was the perfect spot to build his new horse hospital. Doc also perfected his own line of medicines, including Keystone Liniment, which could be used to treat both horses and people.

After the war, many formerly enslaved people faced racism and prejudice from white people who would not recognize them as equals. Doc decided that the best way to beat the prejudice he encountered was to try and make friends with everyone and show them he could be a successful businessman. He eventually opened a blacksmith shop, a wagon wheel–and–harness-making shop, a restaurant, and a hotel. He even built a racetrack and dreamed of raising fine racehorses of his own.

Doc's Keystone Liniment became so popular that he bought a medicine wagon, hired entertainers, and hit the road. He sold his medicines in towns across the South. Soon Doc was one of the wealthiest men in Shelbyville.

One day as Doc and his wagon clattered through a dusty town, he heard about a rundown circus in Tupelo, Mississippi, that was trying to sell its horses. As he neared the ragtag circus, Doc spotted a scrawny gray mare. She looked neglected and abused, and she walked with a limp. Despite her sad condition, Doc recognized that the mare was a purebred Arabian, a horse breed prized for its intelligence and speed.

Doc bought the horse, named Lauretta, for forty dollars and welcomed her into his family.

Doc lovingly nursed Lauretta back to health. When she was strong again, he paired her with one of the fastest racing stallions in the country. Doc hoped their offspring would grow up to be a champion racehorse.

But on that spring day in 1889, the sight of the sickly colt almost broke Doc's heart. In an instant, Doc's racing dreams for the newborn horse vanished.

For weeks the young horse could barely walk. Friends urged Doc to put the colt out of his misery, but Doc wouldn't listen. Just as he had nursed Lauretta back to health, Doc vowed to help her colt. He dished out just the right food and medicines. He massaged the colt's knobby legs, groomed his scraggly coat, and mulled over the perfect name to give him. The biblical name Doc had chosen for a racehorse didn't fit the wobbly youngster, so Doc just called him Jim—Jim Key.

Under Doc's care, Jim's health improved, and his curiosity grew. Jim seemed to study Doc's every move, even when Doc played with his dog. Then one day, Jim zigzagged over with a stick dangling from his mouth. Doc laughed and tossed the stick away. Jim stumbled after it like a clumsy dog.

"He was a knowing colt, I tell you," Doc said. "He showed me he could fetch, and proceeded to try to do the other tricks the dog could do." Jim learned to sit, play dead, act sick, and roll over on cue.

When Jim was about a year old, Lauretta died. Doc was heartbroken, but he also worried about Jim. The orphaned colt needed looking after night and day. So Doc coaxed Jim up the porch steps and through the front door of his house. The young horse made himself right at home.

When Doc counted money, Jim watched. When Doc wrote letters, Jim watched. When Doc opened and closed drawers, Jim watched. "Pretty soon, he began to pick at me, trying to imitate me," Doc said.

In time Jim's legs straightened and he muscled up. He grew into a handsome young stallion—and too big for the house.

Doc knew it was time for his four-legged house guest to move back to the stable. But Jim kicked up a mighty ruckus until Doc started sleeping on a cot next to Jim's stall. Then Doc moved in his desk and most of his office. Before long he was practically living in the stable with Jim.

When Doc was ready to hitch up the medicine wagon again, he decided to bring Jim along as his newest attraction. Doc held up a bottle of Keystone Liniment and announced for people to gather around. He told the crowd how his sickly, crippled colt had grown strong and healthy. Right on cue, Jim pretended to be sick. He limped and drooped and snorted and wobbled. Then Doc gave Jim a spoonful of medicine and massaged a dollop of liniment into his legs. Suddenly Jim acted well again. He pranced around, frisky as a pup.

The audience clapped and laughed and lined up to buy Doc's medicines.

Back at home one day, Doc's wife walked into the stable, munching on a snack.

"Jim, do you want a piece of apple?" she asked. Jim nodded his head up and down. Mrs. Key ran back to the house calling, "Doctor, Doctor, the horse can say yes!"

Doc began to wonder what else his horse could learn.

The stable was transformed into a horse-sized classroom. Doc painted sugar on a cardboard square marked with the letter *A* and held it up to Jim.

"A, A, A," Doc said. Jim swiveled his ears and listened. Then he licked the card until it was soggy.

Doc created a new card out of tin. Every day he patiently repeated "A, A, A" as he slipped the card between Jim's lips. For weeks Jim just licked the sugar and stared blankly at his teacher. Doc sighed and shook his head, but kept at it.

After six months Jim finally understood. If Doc called for the letter *A*, Jim grabbed the right card and dropped it into Doc's hand. In no time Jim learned to fetch the *B* card, then the C card, then all the way to the *Z* card. Doc was proud. He rewarded Jim with an apple or a sugar cube for each correct answer.

Next Doc had Jim combine letters to spell words, choose numbers to make sums, find flags to identify states, move clock hands to tell time, and a whole lot more.

When it was time for Jim to learn to write, Doc painted Jim's name with sugar on a blackboard. It took months for the horse to learn to lick the pattern of his name. Then Doc slipped some chalk between Jim's teeth so the horse could write his name. The chalk crumbled. They needed a bigger piece.

Seven years passed quickly in Jim's private classroom. The more kindness Doc heaped on Jim, the more willing the horse was to learn.

Doc was now ready to show the world what Jim could do.

Their chance came in 1897, at the Tennessee Centennial Exposition, a huge fair held in Nashville. Doc Key had been asked to help plan a building where African Americans could showcase their art, culture, and inventions.

Doc asked the fair directors if he could exhibit Jim. At first the directors laughed. A horse that could read, spell, write, and do sums? Ridiculous! But as one of the organizers of the fair, Doc insisted that Jim have a stage of his own.

Soon visitors were strolling past the giant seesaw and past Edison's new moving picture machine to see Jim. Throughout the fairgrounds, people chattered about the remarkable educated horse.

During one special show, Doc greeted the packed crowd, then turned to Jim.
"Jim, can you show me where President McKinley sits today?" Doc asked.
Jim strutted to center stage, faced the president of the United States, and
bowed. Then Jim walked over to the card rack, scanned the name cards, and
picked out the one marked "McKinley." A gasp echoed through the room.

Audience members began shouting out requests for Jim. "Spell this word." "Divide these numbers." "Get that card." "File that letter." "Ring up this sale." Jim did it all without a mistake. He even wrote his name on the blackboard: J-I-M K-E-Y.

People couldn't believe their eyes. How could a horse learn to do such things?

"The whip makes horses stubborn and they obey through fear," Doc explained. "Kindness, kindness, and more kindness, that's the way."

After the Tennessee Centennial Exposition, Doc and Jim went on the road again. This time they had a big-time promoter, Albert Rogers, to arrange performances for them. News of Jim's remarkable skills spread across the country. Admiring reporters began calling the horse Beautiful Jim Key. The name stuck.

Doc and Beautiful Jim Key performed around the country, but the farther south they traveled, the more racial discrimination Doc faced. Often he wasn't allowed to eat in the same restaurants, sleep in the same hotels, or ride in the same railroad cars as white people.

Sometimes Doc and Jim weren't allowed to perform because people didn't believe Doc's claims of his horse's skills. When Doc offered to perform for schools in Cincinnati, Ohio, a school board member replied, "We can't close our schools for horse shows." And people who didn't know about Doc's gentle training methods worried that Jim might be an abused horse performing out of fear.

After a while, Doc and Jim caught the attention of humane societies, groups of people who were committed to ending cruelty toward animals. Like Doc, members of the humane societies believed that animals were intelligent, capable of emotions, and willing to learn if treated well. They deserved protection. Beautiful Jim Key was the perfect animal to represent their cause.

A portion of the ticket sales for Jim's performances was donated to the humane societies. The money was used to buy horse ambulances and rescue cranes, fund educational programs, and buy books about animals for libraries. With their growing fame, Doc and Jim were helping to promote the cause of kindness toward animals.

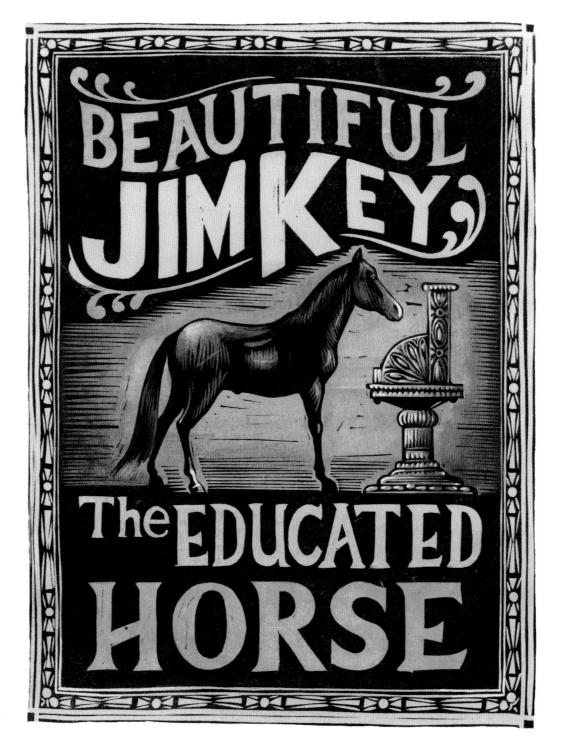

Albert Rogers worked hard to get Doc and Jim onto prestigious stages. In New York, they performed in their own Broadway play, *The Scholar and a Model Office Boy*. Jim played the parts of a student and a clerk. He answered the phone, rang school bells, identified colors, made change from a cash register, filed letters, and more.

At a performance in St. Louis, Jim showed off his math skills. A man called out, "Jim if you take seven, multiply it by three, add nine, divide by three, and subtract seven, what should the answer be?"

Jim paused for a moment, then picked up the card marked with a "3."

The man jumped to his feet. "You're wrong, Jim," he shouted. "The answer is seven."

Jim shook his head. No, no, no. The audience hurried to do the math. It turned out that Jim was correct. The answer was three.

People asked Doc if any horse could learn the skills Jim had mastered. He said yes, "providing he has not been abused."

By 1898, school districts around the country had decided that Doc Key and Beautiful Jim Key were perfect examples of education and kindness. They canceled school days so students could see Jim perform.

Children lined up to compete in spelling bees against the "most highly educated horse in the world." In St. Louis, Missouri, Jim won by spelling the word *R-E-V-E-L-A-T-I-O-N*. In Minneapolis, Minnesota, he won with the name I-S-A-I-A-H. In Baltimore, Maryland, he won by spelling the word *P-H-Y-S-I-C-S*. Other cities came up with different words to test Jim. Most times, Jim won.

Around the United States, about two million children stepped right up to sign the official Jim Key Pledge: "I promise always to be kind to animals."

Doc Key and Beautiful Jim Key were now famous. Record-breaking crowds packed coliseums, theaters, and music halls across the nation to see them. In every city and town, thousands of people bought tickets to attend Doc and Jim's performances. Sometimes police officers had to step in to control the mobs of enthusiastic fans who gathered.

Doc and Jim were invited to perform on stages where only white entertainers had been welcome before. Doc would not accept the segregated seating that forced African Americans into the worst seats. He insisted on special performances with equal seating for all. The property owners agreed. They couldn't argue with the most popular attraction in the country.

In spite of Jim's many skills, skeptics tried to prove that Doc and Jim's act was all a hoax. They scrambled the letters, mixed up the numbers, scattered the colors and flags. Nothing seemed to fool Jim. In 1901, an investigation was conducted by professors from Harvard University. They studied Doc and Jim's performances looking for signs of trickery. They asked Doc many questions.

"Some say it's hypnotism and that kind of thing, but I don't know anything about that," Doc said. "But I do know Jim knows and does what I ask him to do."

The next day the *Boston Daily Globe* newspaper printed an article with the results of the Harvard study. The professors came to the conclusion that there were no tricks or hoax. "It is simply education," they said.

By 1906, seventy-three-year-old Doc and seventeen-year-old Jim were worn out. For nine years they had traveled the country. Now it was time to go home to the rolling hills of Shelbyville, where they could continue to learn and play together. They had proven to millions of people what Doc Key had always believed: with kindness, anything is possible.

"It is hoped that those who have met Jim Key will have carried away with them a kinder regard toward animals and will go forth resolved to whatever may be in their power for the care of our . . . friends."

—from "A Tribute to Jim Key," *Atlanta Constitution*, December 23, 1898

Afterword

William "Doc" Key, ca. 1900

William "Doc" Key was born in Winchester, Tennessee. His exact year of birth is unknown, although several historical documents support 1833, which is also the date on his gravestone. When William was a small child, he and his enslaved family were inherited by John W. Key of Shelbyville, Tennessee. As was the custom, William was given his master's last name. Although he was enslaved, William had a surprisingly close relationship with the Key family, perhaps because John Key's uncle may have been William's father, making John and William cousins. William was encouraged in his studies and is believed to have sometimes joined the Keys' sons, who were younger than him, for lessons. William was also allowed to travel alone, away from the Keys' farm, to provide medical care to other enslaved people and to help with animals. We may never know the entire story, but years later Doc remarked, "I was one of those fortunate men who had a kind master."

When the Civil War broke out in 1861, two of the Keys' sons, Merit and Alexander, joined the Confederate army, followed later by John F., their younger brother. William, known by then as Doc, was opposed to helping the forces that could ensure the continuation of slavery. But he felt a duty to keep the Keys' sons safe, so he followed them to war.

Doc was among thousands of African Americans who served on the Confederate side in noncombat roles such as servants, cooks, and laborers. Because of his skills, Doc worked as a medic and surgeon, treating wounded Confederate soldiers and horses. Sometimes he was given a temporary pass to return home. Doc used these opportunities to help enslaved people escape to freedom along the Underground Railroad.

Most of the enslaved people in Tennessee gained their freedom during the Civil War while the state was under Union control. Once free, Doc was eager to support the Union cause. He acted as a guide, sneaking Union soldiers into Confederate camps. He was captured twice by Union officers and accused of being a spy. Each time Doc narrowly escaped execution.

When the war ended in 1865, Doc delivered the Keys' sons safely home. Now a free man, Doc

worked hard and saved his money. Despite having no formal education, within a few years he became a wealthy and respected businessman. As his business interests grew, his farm and household grew too. Doc was married four times. Sadly, his first three wives died. Although he had no children of his own, extended family members frequently lived in Doc's house, until he built a second home for them on his property.

Doc read widely, took a keen interest in politics, and became a self-taught veterinarian. *Bell's Handbook to Veterinary Homeopathy* was among the resources he turned to when working with animal patients. His greatest financial success was Keystone Liniment, a medicine he formulated. Doc frequently traveled around the country with his medicine wagon, lecturing on horses and selling his liniment. To draw crowds, he sometimes brought along black entertainers, plus a pet monkey and a pony that he had taught to perform tricks. It was during one of these trips that Doc purchased Lauretta, Jim Key's mother.

Lauretta was claimed to be the purest Arabian in the world, the "Queen of Horses." As the story goes, she was stolen from a Persian sheikh and first sold to circus founder P. T. Barnum for around fifty thousand dollars. Eventually Lauretta was sold to poorer circuses that abused and neglected her. According to Albert Rogers, Doc and Jim's promoter, Doc found Lauretta in Mississippi. After Doc nursed her back to health, he took Lauretta along with his medicine show. He claimed she was the smartest horse he had ever known. When her colt was born, Doc had little hope for the wobbly youngster. Little did he know that he and Jim would change the world.

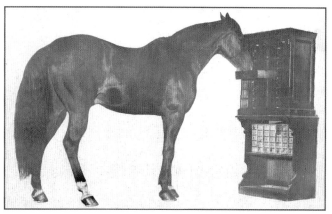

Jim Key filing letters in a mail cabinet

Doc and Beautiful Jim Key's performances far exceeded those mentioned in this book. Jim counted with his hoof, made change from a cash register, operated a crank organ and a telephone, and told time. He identified playing cards, money, colors, flags, and Bible passages. He filed letters in alphabetical order and pulled items from a storage trunk at Doc's request. Jim's most celebrated trick was to retrieve a silver dollar from a bucket of water without drinking a drop. The horse also appeared to have a sense of humor. When Doc teased about selling him, Jim teetered and limped and acted like he was dying—until Doc announced he had changed his mind!

The Tennessee Centennial Exposition of 1897 featured a grand building called the Negro Building, where Jim performed. At the time, the word *Negro*, which means "black" in Spanish and Portuguese, was used to refer to people of African descent; but today the accepted terms are African American and

black. After President McKinley raved to the press about Jim's performance at the exposition, Albert Rogers introduced himself to Doc. As a promoter of amusement acts and a philanthropist interested in humane causes, Rogers was an ideal partner for Doc. Rogers was also able to gain Doc and Jim access to stages that did not normally allow African American performers.

Audiences were always stunned by Jim's intelligence. Notable guests at Jim's shows included educator Booker T. Washington, bandleader John Philip Sousa, future president William H. Taft, and Alice Roosevelt, daughter of President Theodore Roosevelt. Yet throughout their career, Doc and Jim continued to face skeptics. No evidence of trickery was ever discovered, but some people believed that Doc either hypnotized Jim or used subtle body language and other cues to direct Jim's responses. Although we still can't explain many of Jim's apparent skills, it is remarkable that the horse rarely made a mistake. Once a reporter showed up at Jim's stall unannounced and asked to test Jim in private, but the man did not have an apple in his pocket to give Jim as a reward. When Doc returned and asked Jim how it went, the horse spelled out the word *F-R-U-I-T-L-E-S-S.*

Entrance to Jim Key's Silver Horseshoe Pavilion, Louisiana Purchase Exposition, St. Louis, 1904

Jim Key with Doc Key and Monk (on chair)

During their travels, Doc found a scruffy, stray dog with an injured foot. He brought the dog home, tended to its wounds, and named the dog Monk. Monk and Jim became inseparable friends. The

dog enjoyed sitting on Jim's back and served as the horse's personal bodyguard.

Jim was a pampered celebrity, but for many animals, the nineteenth century was an especially cruel time. Thousands of streetcar horses died every year from overwork and mistreatment. Too often, people took out their frustrations and anger on large and small animals, believing they could not think, reason, or feel pain. In 1866, Henry Bergh founded the American Society for the Prevention of Cruelty to Animals (ASPCA). In 1868, George Angell founded the Massachusetts SPCA and later the American Humane Education Society. More humane societies followed. Each organization gained supporters once Doc and Jim showed that kindness was a more powerful tool than cruelty when training animals. George Angell awarded Beautiful Jim Key the Living Example Award. Doc was awarded the Service to Humanity Award, a gold medal inscribed "Glory to God, Peace on Earth, Kindness to All Harmless Living Creatures."

Over the course of nine years of performing, approximately ten million people witnessed the loving bond between Doc and Jim. Money from ticket sales helped support humane societies across the United States. Among other activities, these organizations enforced anticruelty laws and began sheltering homeless animals. People noticed, and began to change the way they treated animals.

Doc and Jim lived out their days on Doc's Shelbyville, Tennessee, farm. Doc died in 1909 and is buried at the Willow Mount Cemetery in Shelbyville. Jim remained in the care of veterinarian Stanley Davis, but the horse's health declined rapidly after the loss of his lifelong friend. In 1912, at the age of twenty-three, Jim died in the front yard of Doc's house. Today a humble memorial marker near Shelbyville pays tribute to Jim and his friends: Doc, Albert Rogers, and Monk.

Doc Key and Beautiful Jim Key

Doc and Jim's legacy lives on in today's stronger humane movement, better enforced animal anticruelty laws, and greater societal compassion toward animals. But the fight to end cruelty is an ongoing battle. Beautiful Jim Key is a reminder to all of Doc Key's enduring message—that each of us should step right up and choose kindness.

Quotation Sources

p. 4: "He's the . . . did see." Doc Key, quoted in Albert R. Rogers, *The Story of Beautiful Jim Key: The Most Wonderful Horse in All the World* (Charleston, SC: Nabu Press, 2010), p. 7.

p. 16: "He was . . . tell you." Doc Key, quoted in Mim Eichler Rivas, *Beautiful Jim Key: The Lost History of a Horse and a Man Who Changed the World* (New York: William Morrow, 2005), p. 40.

"He showed . . . could do." Ibid.

p. 18: "Pretty soon . . . imitate me." Doc Key, quoted in Essie Lee Mott, *Beautiful Jim Key: The Wonder of the Age in Animal Education, 1897–1906* (New York: Carlton Press, 1972), p. 41.

p. 22: "Jim . . . of apple?" Doc Key, quoted in Rogers, *The Story of Beautiful Jim Key: The Most Wonderful Horse in All the World*, p. 9.

"Doctor, Doctor . . . say yes!" Ibid.

p. 23: "A, A, A." Doc Key, quoted in "Wonderful Jim Key, The Educated Horse, Being Exhibited by the Humane Society Here" (*Atlanta Constitution*, December 19, 1898).

p. 28: "Jim . . . sits today?" Doc Key, quoted in Rivas, *Beautiful Jim Key: The Lost History of a Horse and a Man Who Changed the World*, p. 115.

p. 29: "The whip . . . through fear." Doc Key, quoted in "The Horse Jim Key: How Dr. Key Taught Him the Alphabet" (*Minneapolis Journal*, November 18, 1899).

"Kindness, kindness . . . the way." Ibid.

p. 31: "We can't . . . horse shows." Quoted in Rogers "Information Regarding Jim Key." Undated letter to unknown recipient (Tennessee State Library and Archives).

p. 35: "Jim if you . . . answer be?" Quoted in "On the Pike: Nothing Too Startling for This Feature of St. Louis Fair" (*Daily Courier*, July 17, 1904).

"You're wrong . . . is seven." Ibid.

"providing . . . abused." Doc Key, quoted in Essie Mott Lee, *The Man Who Educated a Horse: A Pioneer in Humane Education* (Bloomington, IN: 1st Books Library/Author House, 1998), p. 30.

p. 37: "most highly . . . the world." Quoted in "At the Waverly Fair" (*Newark Evening News*, September 9, 1897).

"I promise . . . to animals." Quoted in Lee, *The Man Who Educated a Horse: A Pioneer in Humane Education*, p. 119.

p. 40: "Some say . . . about that." Doc Key, quoted in "Jim Key is Highly Educated—Can Both Spell and Figure" (*Post-Standard*, September 7, 1902).

"But I . . . him to do." Ibid.

p. 41: "It is . . . education." Quoted in Rogers, Jim Key 1901 promotional pamphlet (from *Boston Daily Globe*, October 27, 1901).

p. 43: "It is . . . friends." Quoted in "A Tribute to Jim Key" (*Atlanta Constitution*, December 23, 1898).

p. 44: "I was . . . kind master." Doc Key, quoted in Rivas, *Beautiful Jim Key: The Lost History of a Horse and a Man Who Changed the World*, p. 47.

Author's Sources

Books

Bedford County Historical Society. *Postcard Memories of Bedford County, Tennessee: Bicentennial Celebration 2007*. Shelbyville, TN: Bedford County Historical Society, 2006.

Beers, Diane L. *For the Prevention of Cruelty: The History and Legacy of Animal Rights Activism in the United States*. Athens, OH: Ohio University Press/Swallow Press, 2006.

Bekoff, Marc. *The Emotional Lives of Animals: A Leading Scientist Explores Animal Joy, Sorrow, and Empathy—And Why They Matter*. Novato, CA: New World Library, 2007.

Cimprich, John. *Slavery's End in Tennessee, 1861–1865*. Tuscaloosa, AL: University of Alabama Press, 1985.

Lee, Essie Mott. *The Man Who Educated a Horse: A Pioneer in Humane Education*. Bloomington, IN: 1st Books Library/Author House, 1998.

Loeper, John J. *Crusade for Kindness: Henry Bergh and the ASPCA*. New York: Atheneum, 1991.

McNamara, Brooks. *Step Right Up: An Illustrated History of the American Medicine Show*. Garden City, NY: Doubleday, 1976.

Mott, Essie Lee. *Beautiful Jim Key: The Wonder of the Age in Animal Education, 1897–1906*. New York: Carlton Press, 1972.

Rivas, Mim Eichler. *Beautiful Jim Key: The Lost History of a Horse and a Man Who Changed the World*. New York: William Morrow, 2005.

Rogers, Albert R. *The Story of Beautiful Jim Key: The Most Wonderful Horse in All the World*. Charleston, SC: Nabu Press, 2010. (reprint of public domain material)

Senour, Caro Smith. *Master St. Elmo, the Autobiography of a Celebrated Dog*. University of California Libraries, 1904.

Newspapers

Age-Herald (Birmingham, AL) "Interest Revived in Humane Work: Jim Key May Cause Reorganization of Local Society." April 6, 1900.

Atlanta Constitution (Atlanta, GA). "A Famous Veterinary Surgeon." April 10, 1876.

———. "A Tribute to Jim Key." December 23, 1898.

———. "A Wonderful Success: Which Has Attended a Worthy Colored Man." February 27, 1881.

———. "Wonderful Jim Key, The Educated Horse, Being Exhibited by the Humane Society Here." December 19, 1898.

Bedford Daily Mail (Bedford, IN). "Wonderful Horse: Taught by an Ex-Slave to Distinguish Letters of Alphabet." December 27, 1897.

Bedford Gazette (Bedford, PA). "On the Pike. Meeting of Two Famous Educators at the Fair: Patience and Kindness." July 15, 1904.

Bee (Earlington, KY). "The Exposition: Splendid Musical Attractions. 'Jim Key the Wonderful Horse.'" June 3, 1897.

Boston Daily Globe (Boston, MA). "Beautiful Jim Key: Horse that Reads, Writes and Changes Money." October 24, 1901.

Daily Courier (Connellsville, PA). "On the Pike: Nothing Too Startling for This Feature of St. Louis Fair." July 17, 1904.

Kansas City Journal (Kansas City, MO). "J. M. Key, Educated Horse: Trained by a 'Voodoo' Doctor for Eight Patient Years." August 22, 1897.

Key, John F. "A Master's Tribute to a Slave of Ante-bellum Days." *Washington Times*, July 13, 1903.

Marion Daily Star (Marion, OH). "He Can Do Almost Anything Except Talk Politics." December 29, 1897.

Minneapolis Journal. (Minneapolis, MN). "Children Will Join in War on Cruelty: Youth of Minneapolis Will Swear to Protect Dumb Animals as Members of Jim Key Bands of Mercy." April 1, 1906.

———. "Jim Key Delights First Night Crowd." April 6, 1906.

———. "Jim Key Does Sums for 8,000 Children." April 4, 1906.

———. "Jim Key's Mascot Was Once a Common Stray Dog." April 3, 1906.

———. "The Horse Jim Key: How Dr. Key Taught Him the Alphabet." November 18, 1899.

Newark Evening News (Newark, NJ). "At the Waverly Fair." September 9, 1897.

New York Times (New York, NY). "Jim Key A Clever Horse." December 1, 1897.

Post-Standard (Syracuse, NY). "Jim Key is Highly Educated—Can Both Spell and Figure." September 7, 1902.

San Antonio Daily Light (San Antonio, TX). "How Intelligent Horse is Trained to do Tricks." October 21, 1906.

Times-Dispatch (Richmond, VA). "Faithful to Old Master: Remarkable Case of the Devotion of a Negro Slave." July 28, 1903.

Waterloo Daily Courier (Waterloo, IA). "An Equine Wonder: Marvelous Exhibition Given by a Horse in Kansas City." March 21, 1906.

York Daily (York, PA). "The King of All Horses, Beautiful Jim Key." October 4, 1898.

Websites and Other Sources

Beautiful Jim Key. http://www.beautifuljimkey.com.

Rogers, Albert R. "Information Regarding Jim Key." Undated letter to unknown recipient (after the deaths of Doc Key and Jim Key).

———. Jim Key promotional pamphlets. Various editions, 1897–1906.

Tennessee State Library and Archives. "The Beautiful Jim Key Collection." http://sos.tn.gov/products/tsla/beautiful-jim-key-collection.

———. "The Beautiful Jim Key Collection." Microfilm roll AC#1888-1.

———. "The Beautiful Jim Key Collection." Physical scrapbooks.

van Zelm, Antionette G. "Hope Within a Wilderness of Suffering: The Transition from Slavery to Freedom During the Civil War and Reconstruction in Tennessee." http://www.tn4me.org/pdf/TransitionfromSlaverytoFreedom.pdf.